HOW TO EMBARRASS GROWN-UPS

Paul Cookson has b_____ _____ _sing grown-ups for many years now by maki_____ _____ __th his poems and do daft action_____ _____ _____ __arents and teachers loc_____ _____ _____ en he picks on them for_____ _____ _____ _ words like 'snog' and 'knicke__ _____ _____ teachers love it too, especially when he e__ _____ he head teacher and deputy head.

When he is working with David Harmer as Spill the Beans, they are able to embarrass twice as many grown-ups – which is great fun. Paul and David are embarrassing grown-ups – especially to their families, who wish they would stop being silly in public.

David Parkins *is* a grown-up. Well, he's old. He is also an embarrassment. He wears ink-spattered shirts and very old shoes. I mean, *HONESTLY!* He embarrasses himself and he embarrasses his eight-year-old daughter. *And* he sings in the street.

HOW TO EMBARRASS GROWN-UPS

Poems chosen by
Paul Cookson

*Illustrated by **David Parkins***

MACMILLAN CHILDREN'S BOOKS

Dedicated to David – fellow Bean,
Good friend, good poet, good times ahead.

First published 2004 by Macmillan Children's Books
a division of Macmillan Publishers Limited
20 New Wharf Road, London N1 9RR
Basingstoke and Oxford
www.panmacmillan.com

Associated companies throughout the world

ISBN 0 330 41032 6

5 7 9 8 6

A CIP catalogue record for this book is available from
the British Library.

Printed and bound in Great Britain by Mackays of Chatham plc, Kent

Contents

Embarrassing Grown-Ups in Public

Snogging each other in front of your friends
Pretending that they can keep up with the trends
Giving loud kisses in crowded places
Using their hankies to wipe your faces
Embarrassing grown-ups in public

Telling your auntie what Dad really said
Staring at strangers while shaking your head
Asking rude questions in overloud voices
Spitting and sneezing and other rude noises
Embarrassing grown-ups in public

Holding your hand while walking round town
The lick and the spit to keep your hair down
When Dad thinks he's Elvis and Mum thinks she's Britney
Squeezing in clothes saying, 'Yes they still fit me!'
Embarrassing grown-ups in public

Remarking at volume how you need the loo
Hopping around like a drunk kangaroo
Enquiring how to spell diarrhoea
Folding and moulding the wax from your ear
Embarrassing grown-ups in public

Falling asleep and dribbling on trains
When Dad blows his nose and looks at the stains
Bad made up jokes that have them in stitches
Gran's washing line bloomers creating eclipses
Embarrassing grown-ups in public

Asking if Dad's 'little problem' has gone
Asking your grandad where babies come from
Laughing at rude bits on nudes in museums
Pointing and asking if Granny can see 'em
Embarrassing grown-ups in public

As bad as each other so share out the blame
Children and adults behave just the same
Causing embarrassment, redness and shame
They naturally seem to share the same aim
Embarrassing grown-ups in public!

Paul Cookson

The Paint Job

I'm watching the television
Dad is snoring on the settee
Mum's out at work and the twins
play with their face paints at the table.
Now Dad's snores are getting louder
rumbling round the room
like a hundred motorbikes
his chin is beginning to wobble
his mouth sags open
the blue glare of the television
bounces off his shiny bald head.

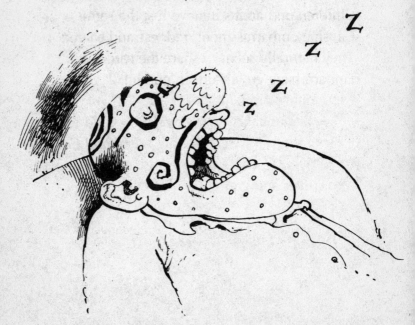

I have an idea, a very big idea
an idea so big
it makes me snort with laughter
I quietly stand and tiptoe
towards the twins, whisper, 'Shush,'
put my finger to my lips and grin
pick up a few of their tubes of face paint
start to work on my creation
they watch, eyes wide with excitement.

To start with I draw
a set of circles on Dad's head
a blue one with a white one inside it
then a small red one
with a brown splodge in the middle
so now he looks a bit like a target.
Next his eyes get some giant black glasses
a bright purple moustache
sprouts under his nose, which is yellow.
Dad soon has a rash of big orange spots
all over his cheeks as well as some streaks
of silver and grey round his chin.

He looks quite a sight and we start to giggle
he suddenly wakes and we jump back.
'Your mum!' he shouts. 'I'm meant to meet her
right now, after work, to go to the pictures!'

He dashes off out of the door
runs down the road as we wave goodbye
then fall in a heap of helpless laughter
and wonder how quickly they'll be coming home.

David Harmer

That Word

is the naughtiest word on Neptune,
you mustn't repeat it in space.
　　And if, one afternoon,
you meet the Man in the Moon,
　　beg you, don't say it to his face.

It'll turn the air blue on Pluto,
it's a mucky word on Mercury and Mars,
　　What you say down here,
　　let me make it clear,
is not what you say among the stars.

I swear it's a swear word on Saturn,
they think it's a vile term on Venus,
　　it's enough to put a curse
　　on the whole universe
and they'll all cover their ears on Uranus.

You can say it in Cardiff or Cairo,
you can bellow it all round Bengal,
　　and if, by some chance,
　　you should shout it in France,
you'll find it's not naughty at all.

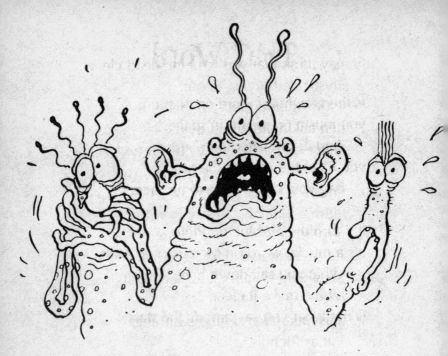

But you'll alienate every alien
if you use it when chatting to them.
   So if one of them says, 'Hey,
      what did you just say?'
say, 'Nothing. I'd a small bit of phlegm.'

You may think that you're being dead clever,
or sophisticated saying it, but
    it's a word you must avoid
    when talking to an asteroid.
Say it once and at once they'll 'Tut-tut.'

It can make them gasp 'Oh!' in a UFO,
it can turn a black hole deathly white.
    If a Martian adult
    used such an insult,
the stars would switch off for the night.

Now this little poem's just a warning,
accept it as friendly advice,
    but if, one rash minute,
    it slips out on some planet,
for heaven's sake don't say it twice!

                                    David Horner

Good Questions to Ask When Visitors Come

Where has all our dust gone?
It's just not fair!
All my friends' phone numbers
Were written there.

Why are we at the table?
I'd rather eat my tea
Watching TV programmes
On the living room settee.

Who's been in the cupboard under the stairs
And dug out those ugly plaster geese?
You said they should be dropped off a cliff –
So why are they on the mantelpiece?

Why has Mum gone very pale?
And why is Dad so red?
Why is it whenever visitors come
That I get sent to bed?

Jan Dean

Introducing Dad

If I may, Miss
I'd like to introduce my dad
Mum left us last year
And that made him really sad
He told me you were pretty
And his favourite colour's beige
And it isn't that uncommon
To date women half your age
And we all know that he's bald
Beneath that funny flick of hair
You just have to humour him
And pretend his hair's all there
His feet smell a bit funny
And his brain's a trifle slow
And you haven't got a boyfriend, Miss
So . . . could you please give Dad a go?

Roger Stevens

Dad's Birthday Gift

Every year
Gran buys Dad a tie.
Every year
Dad says,
'This is worse than
last year's.
It looks like
her mangy cat's been sick over it.'

Every year
We go to Gran's for birthday tea.
Every year
Dad shows off the new tie.
Every year
Gran says,
'I never know what to buy you.'
Every year
Dad says,
'You can never have enough ties.'

But this year
My little brother says,
'Gran, is your cat feeling better?
Because Dad said it must have been sick on his
    new tie.'

John Coldwell

Used Ink

William Shakespeare used ink (*used ink*),
when he penned his many plays.

School children once used ink (*used ink*),
and feathered quills, in olden days.

Used ink (*used ink*), used ink (*used ink*),
used ink (*used ink*), used ink (*used ink*).

Doctor Addicott used ink (*used ink*),
on her prescription for Gran's warts.

Our teachers all used ink (*used ink*),
to write our school reports.

Used ink (*used ink*), used ink (*used ink*),
used ink (*used ink*), used ink (*used ink*).

Last year's Valentines used ink (*used ink*),
to say, 'I ♥ U true.'

My word processor used ink (*used ink*),
to print this just for you.

Used ink (*used ink*), used ink (*used ink*),
used ink (*used ink*), used ink (*used ink*).

Mike Johnson

Victoria's Poem

Send me upstairs without any tea,
refuse me a plaster to stick on my knee.

Make me kiss Grandpa who smells of his pipe,
make me eat beetroot, make me eat tripe.

Throw all my best dolls into the river.
Make me bacon and onions – with liver.

Tell Mr Allan I've been a bad girl,
          Rename me Nellie, rename me
               Pearl.

          But don't, even if
               the world suddenly ends,
                    ever again, Mother,

                         wipe my face with
                              a tissue
                         in front of my
                              friends.

Fred Sedgwick

Moments

A most embarrassing moment.
The postman looked into the room,
Saw Mother rock-and-rolling –
Her partner a dust-filled broom.

John Kitching

Our Strictest Teacher

Our strictest teacher
Thought he'd done well
Trying to work a spell
With his
Deep
Dark
Commanding voice
Leaving us no choice
But to obey.
Sorry! No way!
Soon fixed that . . .

His tone's now a
silly 'un
Cos we filled his inhaler
With extra strong helium.

Ian Corns

Talk Properly!

I drank this funny liquid,
It went straight to my head.
I couldn't believe
The words that I then said.
'Pass the milk'
Was 'Mass the pilk'
And
'Tan I have more coast?
Can't bind my fag,
I'll biss the mus'
And
'Here's the porning most.'
Once at school
Things got worse,
Especially in the hall.
'Mood gorning beveryody,
Sice to nee you all.'
All day long
It went like this,
Not a happy feature,
Particularly as I am
Hatherside's Head Teacher.

Redvers Brandling

Bald as an Egg, or Egg on Your Face

The four of us, in a café,
Dad, Mum, my brother, and me,
Eating egg, beans, bacon,
Sausage, and chips, for tea,

When suddenly my brother,
Sitting in his high chair,
Bawls out across the café
'That man got no hair.'

All heads jerk sideways.
Eyeballs protrude to stare
At a gent in a dark-blue blazer.
'That man got no hair'

Screeches my wretched brother
While ketchup runs down his leg,
Till Mum succeeds in shushing him
With a spoonful of fried egg.

When we slink out of the café,
Ashamed of my brother's disgrace,
The bald gent says to my mother
'That child's got egg on his face.'

Leo Aylen

Inspection

So let me get this right, Miss.

When the inspectors come to our class

You want me to stand on a table
And yell at the top of my voice
Leap on to a group of children
Who are working cooperatively
And smash their DT model to pieces?

You require me to run at great speed
Around the edges of the class
Ripping down all of those perfect displays
You've recently put up
For the benefit of the inspection team?

You need me to dive into the book corner
Sending hundreds of volumes
Of carefully ordered texts
Go flying in a thousand different directions
And disturbing those who are reading quietly
    and sensibly within?

You expect me to grab fistfuls
Of indelible markers
And selecting the brashest colours
Scrawl metre-high swear words
All over the classroom walls?

Miss, what's that funny look on your face?
Have I got the wrong idea?

Jonny Zucker

Teacher Beware

As a poem you may read out in class
I feel I must make myself clear.
You see, sometimes I break the rules
and say something really rude.
Don't blame me. I can't help it.
I'm just making myself up as I go.
I mean, be fair, how do I know
what's going to come next?
I know what you're thinking,
you wish you hadn't started me now –
but you can't stop, can you?
What will the class think?
Oh dear, you're flushing.
Can you feel your scalp prickle with heat?
Are your toes curling like snails
trying to tuck their heads in?
You're in trouble now, and it's not my fault.
I told you what I'm like.
Yes, I know, for you it's no fun.
Is that why you're clenching the cheeks of your
face.
Phew! That was close. I bet you thought I was going
   to say BUM.

Stephen Clarke

A Night With the Girls

A night with the 'girls' –
Mum couldn't wait.
She was so excited –
in a right state.

She'd bought some new shoes
and a dress to wear,
spent ages with make-up
and fiddling with her hair.

We settled down
with some fish and chips
in front of the telly
to watch The Premiership.

'Well – how d'it go?'
we asked when she came in.
'You two might've told me
I still had curlers in!'

Jill Townsend

Daddy, it's Only a Game

'Deck that kid!'
'Make him hurt!'
'Push him down!'
'Grab his shirt!'
'Bash the bum!'
'Make him cry!'
'Put an elbow
in his eye!'

Daddy, please, stop shouting,
those words are not OK.
They may have worked when you were young,
but I don't play that way.

You make me feel embarrassed,
and lots and lots of stress.
And, Daddy, please remember . . .

I'm only playing *chess.*

Ted Scheu

Kisses!

Last week
my face was smothered in kisses
Yes – KISSES!

First there was the dribbly-wibbly kiss
when Mum slurped all over me
like an eight-mouthed octopus. ('There's my favourite
    boy!')
Then there was the lipstick-redstick kiss
when my aunty's rosy lips
painted themselves on my cheeks ('Isn't he so
    handsome!'
Next came the flutter-eye, butterfly kiss
when my girlfriend smoochy-cooched
and fluttered her eyelashes at the same time.
    ('OOOOOOOH!')
After that there was the soggy-doggy kiss
when our pet Labrador, Sally
tried to lick my face off. ('Slop! Slop! Woof!')
Following that there was 'watch out here I come'
    miss-kiss
when my little sister aimed for me
but missed and kissed the cat instead.
    ('UUUUUUUUUURGH!')
Then there was the spectacular-Dracula kiss

when my cousin Isabel leaped from behind the
   shower curtain
and attacked my neck ('AAAAAAAAAAGH – suck!')
Of course, there was the 'ssssssssssh don't tell anyone'
   self-kiss
when I looked in the bathroom mirror
and kissed myself. (Once was enough!)

Ian Souter

Why

When grown-ups get embarrassed
they say . . .

I wish the earth would open and swallow me up

or

I didn't know where to put myself

or

I hid my face in shame

or even

I could have died!

So why do they play guitars that aren't there
and dance like chickens trying to fly?

Why do they go to the shops in their slippers
and have Daffy Duck on their ties?

Why do they put concrete gnomes in their gardens
and read the paper while watching the news?

Why do they go on holiday to *get away from it all*
and sit on the motorway in queues?

Why do they go to work all day
and sit there just watching the clock?

Why do they go swimming when they've got a verruca
and wear just one rubber sock?

Stephen Clarke

Probably Our Head's Top 10 Most Embarrassing Memories

The time the cleaner
Ticked him off because of the
Mess in his office.

The time he sat through
Assembly with a kiss of
Lipstick on his cheek.

The time he announced –
Pride comes before a fall! Then
Fell off the school stage.

That sponsored silence
When *he* was the latecomer
With the squeaky shoes.

That parents' night when
His new chair blew raspberries
Whenever he moved.

The moment it dawned
We were spellbound by his wide
Flies – not his wise words.

That prize day when he
Ended up presenting *three*
To his own daughter.

The morning after
Head comes bottom in pub quiz
Made local headlines.

The day he showed us
How to cross safely and got
Hit by a pushbike.

And when we learned that
Once punk rocker, Vicious Vince,
Was none other than . . .

Philip Waddell

Dad, Don't Dance

Whatever you do, don't dance, Dad
Whatever you do, don't dance.
Don't wave your arms
Like a crazy buffoon
Displaying your charms
By the light of the moon
Trying to romance
A lady baboon
Whatever you do, don't dance.

When you try to dance
Your left leg retreats
And your right leg starts to
  advance
Whatever you do, don't
  dance, Dad
Has a ferret crawled into
  your pants?
Or maybe a hill full of ants
Don't Samba
Don't Rumba
You'll tumble
And stumble
Whatever you do, Dad,
  don't dance.

Don't glide up the aisle with a trolley
Or twirl the girl on the till
You've been banned from dancing in Tesco's
Cos your Tango made everyone ill.

Whatever you do, don't dance, Dad
Whatever you do, don't dance.
Don't make that weird face
Like you ate a sour plum
Don't waggle your hips
And stick out your bum
But most of all – PLEASE –
Don't smooch with Mum!
Whatever the circumstance.
Whatever you do –
Dad, don't dance.

Roger Stevens

The Jumper Granny Knitted

The wool is rough and itchy
One sleeve is longer than the other
Teddies on the back
She thinks I am my little brother
It's shapeless and untrendy
Embarrassing, ill-fitted
I'm not going out like that . . .
In the jumper Granny knitted.

Thomas the Tank Engine on the front
Seventeen shades of green
She thinks that I'm still seven
When really I'm thirteen
Every Christmas, every birthday
She really is committed
I'm not going out like that . . .
In the jumper Granny knitted.

Don't worry you'll grow into it
It's the size of a family tent
And I was so much looking forward
To the present that she sent

Pretend that it's just perfect
And smile while teeth are gritted
I'm not going out like that . . .
The jumper Granny knitted.

No way seen in public
For fear of ridicule
Too much humiliation
And never near school
But whenever Granny calls
However wits are pitted
You always have to wear it once . . .
The jumper Granny knitted.

I'm not going out like that
In the jumper Granny knitted
I'd rather go in hiding
But that is not permitted
But you always have to wear it once
Or you may as well admit it . . .
That you hate and cannot stand
It makes you want to vomit and
You'd rather have one second-hand
Than . . . the jumper Granny knitted.

Paul Cookson

Penalty Shot

It was only a kick about in the park
It was only a bit of fun
It really wasn't your fault, Dad
It could have happened to anyone.

You are not as young as you were, Dad
It's a while since you last played the game
And without your Bobby Charlton boots
Well, how can you be the one to blame?

But you can still kick the ball, Dad
That sure was a powerful shot
It was nearly Goal of the Month, Dad
You didn't miss by a lot

The bus driver should have seen it
It was an easy ball to avoid
I don't think the policeman was angry
He was only a trifle annoyed

It was just bad luck that the bus driver swerved
Into the Mayor's Rolls-Royce
With the topspin you cleverly put on the ball
He really had no choice

And when the Rolls smashed into the pet shop
Everyone rallied around
To round up the rabbits and hamsters
And I'm sure that the snake *will* be found.

At least no one was hurt, Dad
So there's no need to be so upset
And on the bright side your penalty shot
Made the front page of the *Gazette*.

Roger Stevens

Mr Jewell the Weekend Fool

My PE teacher Mr Jewell
Is rough and tough and really cool
He's what all boys would like to be
As strong as an ox and as fit as a flea.

He's the kind of bloke, you know the sort
Who's really good at every sport
A hunk that all the girls adore
He has admirers by the score.

So just imagine my surprise
When yesterday with my own eyes
I caught a glimpse of Mr Jewell
Behaving like a proper fool.

Together with a group of mates
While visiting our village fête
Drawn by the sound of a concertina
We gathered by the show arena.

Wearing smocks with coloured bands
And waving hankies in their hands
A group of men jigged merrily
With silver bells tied round their knees.

In amongst this crazy lot
And looking like a perfect clot
Tapping sticks and gaily prancing
Was Mr Jewell, Morris dancing.

He skipped and hopped and yelled, 'Yippee!'
The sight of which astounded me
How could our hunky Mr Cool
Turn into such a weekend fool?

Richard Caley

A Sumo Wrestler Chappy

A sumo wrestler chappy
One day in the ring was unhappy
When thrown to the ground
His mum pinned him down
And in view of the crowd changed his nappy.

Paul Cookson

I've Seen
Mrs Newton's Knickers

You'll never believe what I've seen!
Go on . . . have a guess
I've seen Mrs Newton's knickers
The pairs she wears beneath her dress.

Monday's pair is navy blue and thick
Because she teaches Games.
Tuesday's Science so they're fireproof
From the Bunsen burner's flames.

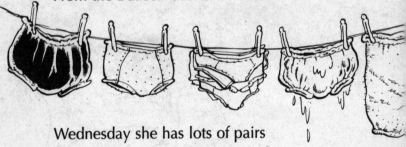

Wednesday she has lots of pairs
To add and take or share in Maths.
Thursday's pair is waterproof
Because of swimming at the baths.

Friday's pair is vast, expansive,
Thermal, flannelette and so
Warming freezing playtime duties
They will reach from head to toe.

Wimbledon or tennis fortnight
Then they're white and rather frilly.
Do not look on April Fool's Day
Because they're very very silly.

Yellow spots, blue polka dots,
Tartan checks, deckchair stripes
But the most amazing pair
Is saved for raves on Saturday nights.

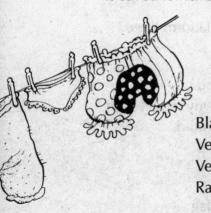

Black and silky, shiny satin,
Very elegant and lacy.
Very brief beyond belief
Rather risqué, really racy.

I've seen Mrs Newton's knickers
Every pattern, each design
Every style in every colour
Hung up on her washing line!

Paul Cookson

In My Bedroom

It's the middle of the night,
Someone's opening my door
And slipping like a snake across
My bedroom floor.

I'm too scared to find out
Who it could be
Until I hear it whisper,
'Cross the bridge for platform three.'

Then I hear a whistle
And a chuff-chuff sound
And the click-clack of my model train
Whizzing round and round.

I flick on the light
To see who's there –
My dad with a green flag
Blinking in the glare

'It's all right, son,
Did I give you a fright?
Just making sure your train set
Is working right.'

John Coldwell

The Wedding

'. . . Therefore, if any man can show any just cause
as to why
they may not lawfully be joined together,
let him speak,
or else hereafter
forever hold his peace.'

'YES!' the best man roared,
with his ear to a radio;
Michael Owen had scored!

Ian Corns

Advice

(after Adrian Mitchell)

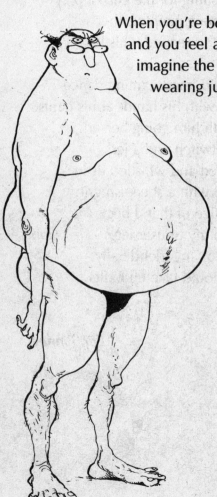

When you're being told off
and you feel all hope has gone
imagine the headmaster
wearing just a purple thong

Dave Calder

Didn't He Dance!

Boy, didn't he dance that day!
Our teacher was whistling for the end of play
And after that penetrating peep
We were waiting for the second whistle
As still as sheep . . .
When he started a wild, mad, ranting dance
Beating and flapping with his hands at his pants.
It went on and on with him going berserk
All of a spasm and a twitch and a jerk.
Well, at last he stopped and whistled us in
And as we went past, with a sheepish grin
He said, 'Take no notice of that, I beg,
I'd just got a wasp up my trouser leg.'
Smart remark to him by my friend Sally:
'Nice one, sir! You should take up ballet.'

Eric Finney

Hello, Mrs Morley

Hello, Mrs Morley, as you can see
There's nobody home now apart from me.
And I can't ask you in for a nice cup of tea
Because Mummy is hiding behind the settee,
And she's not coming out – whatever I say
Until she's quite sure that you've gone away.

One thing, Mrs Morley, before you go,
There's something I really would like to know –
Just what *is* a name-dropping, snooty-nosed cat?
Next door have a Siamese – is it like that?

Jan Dean

The Family Album

No, Mum, don't show her that one.
She won't want to see
photographs of babies
No, that isn't me
Not that baby on the blanket,
legs waving in the air
and with not a stitch of clothes on.
No, Mum, don't you dare . . .
Well that's the end of that then.
Please tell me if I'm silly,
but romance is dead and gone
now that my girlfriend's seen my bum.

Marian Swinger

Pretty Parents

Dad's got tattoos on his chest,
But he's not as bad as Mum.
She's the most embarrassing –
She's got tattoos on her . . . !

Clive Webster

Blackmail

On holiday, my sister,
my mum, my dad and I
were walking down the beach
beneath the Spanish sky
when all at once I saw my teacher
(a horrible surprise)
and my teacher saw me too,
                horror in her eyes
                and grabbed a handy
                beach towel,
                letting out a screech
                for she'd been caught
                out topless,
                topless on the beach.
                As we walked
                away I gloated.
                There was little
                need to mention
                that in future she'd
                think twice
before giving me detention.

Marian Swinger

Dad, You're Not Funny

A few of my mates
Come around to our place
And you're at the door
With a grin on your face.
You know that I know
You're a really good bloke,
But I'll curl up and die
If you tell us a joke.

We don't want to hear
About your days at school,
We don't want to watch
You try to be cool.
We don't want to know
How the world used to be.
We don't want to see
Those videos of me.

We don't want to laugh
At your riddles and rhymes,
At musty old tales
We've heard fifty times.
We don't want a quiz
Where we have to compete,
We don't want to guess
Why the hen crossed the street.

Please don't perform
That ridiculous dance
Like you did on the night
We went out in France.
Don't do impressions
Of pop stars on drugs.
Whatever you do
Don't swamp me with hugs.

So Dad, don't come in,
Your jokes are so dated
I often pretend
That we're not related.
I'd pay you to hide
If I had my own money
The simple truth is –
Dad, you're not funny.

Steve Turner

When Little Billy Burped

When little Billy burped
it rang out like ten bells
with complicated sound effects
and complicated smells.

Some of it was cottage pie
a lot of it was cheese
with a little splash of cabbage
and quite a lot of peas.

With garlic, beans and onions
mixed up in a hurry
a real whiff of fish and chips
a giant wave of curry.

It swirled around our heads
our faces pale and grey
when little Billy burped
and we got in the way.

David Harmer

The I-Spy Book
of Teachers

One point if you catch your teacher yawning,
double that to two if later on you find him snoring,
Three points if you hear your teacher singing

and four if it's a pop song not a hymn.
A generous five points if you ever see him jogging
and six if you should chance upon him snogging.

Seven if you ever find him on his knees and praying
for relief from noisy boys who trouble him.
Eight if you should catch him in the betting shop,

nine if you see him dancing on *Top of the Pops*,
And ten if you hear him say what a lovely class he's got
for then you'll know there's something wrong with him.

Brian Moses

Mum's Mouthfuls

We all know Mum's mouthfuls!

If she wants us to eat something up
she says – 'Go on, have another mouthful.'
Then she ladles out
enough to make a hippopotamus choke
– cabbage, salad, peas, parsnips –
all the grotty stuff
that we normally leave on the plate.
'It's good for you,' she says,
'have another mouthful . . .'

It's always the same.
Mum's idea of what we can cram
in our mouths is way out of line.
'Muesli is good for you,' she says,
'have another mouthful,'
and half the packet appears in the dish.

And then, of course,
when we start to complain she says,
'Don't talk with your mouth full . . .'

But we get our own back . . .
for when Mum's trying to slim
and she says, 'I'll just have a
tiny piece more of that delicious cake.'
We break off a huge slab
and when she complains, we say,
'Mum, it's only a mouthful!'

Brian Moses

The Day My Parents Raced

School Sports Day – and it should have been
A glorious day for me.
I won all four of my events
And our team won – brilliantly!
As the day's best performer
I was chosen to go up
To receive from the headmaster
The special silver cup.
And that was definitely
The high point of my day
Because from that very moment
It was downhill all the way.
They have these Parents' Races:
Gave each dad a skipping rope.
Well, my dad's OK at *running*
But at *skipping*? Not a hope!
You ought to have seen the tangle
He got in – I watched aghast –
Got the rope looped round his ankle,
Blundered on – and came in last.
Things got worse: the Mums' Race,
Just a sixty-metre run,
And there's my mum: tight skirt, daft shoes,

Waiting for the gun.
She looked ridiculous, of course,
But somehow she kept going
And managed to get down the track
Without her knickers showing.
Like Dad, came last, and then collapsed
In a giggling heap, red-faced –
And that's it, that's the story of
The Day My Parents Raced.
Would you say they were embarrassed?
Or Utterly Disgraced?

Eric Finney

My Gran Always Snores

My gran always snores.
How about yours?
She shatters our sleep
And breaks all kinds of laws.
The windows can't hide it,
Nor can the doors.
It's a rumbling racket
That no one adores.
We're all wide awake, when
My grandmother snores.

My gran always snores.
How about yours?
The din makes the dog howl
And shakes all the floors.
The cat tries to cover
Both ears with his paws,
As thunder escapes
From her trembling jaws.
We're all wide awake, when
My grandmother snores.

My gran always snores
How about yours?
I've tried counting sheep,
Gone downstairs, done some chores,
Rubbed cream on my ears
For the blisters and sores,
But nothing, it seems,
Calms the rumpus that pours
Like a flood through the house, when
My grandmother snores.

My gran always snores
How about yours?
I'm thinking of moving
To faraway shores.
I'll walk if I have to,
Or crawl on all fours,
To get me away from
Those deafening roars
That keep us awake when
My grandmother snores.

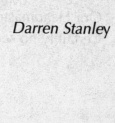

Darren Stanley

Our Head Teacher's Little Secret

It was when we did our class project
About the nineteen seventies . . .

We had to look through old-fashioned books,
Faded newspaper clippings . . .

It was then that we saw it,
The picture that made the front pages . . .

A sunny day at Lords Cricket Ground,
the players, speechless, smiling . . .

A leaping streaker caught forever in mid-air,
Just over the wickets . . .

The hippy hair and beard, but the same sharp nose,
The same black-rimmed glasses . . .

Before we even read the name
We knew just who it was . . .

Our Headmaster's little secret
Certainly no secret any more!

Paul Cookson

You'll Never Guess Who I Met

You'll never guess who I met
You'll never guess who it was
You'll never guess what they said
   About you

Dad, I met someone who knew you
Dad, it was your old teacher from school
Dad, they told me all sorts
   About you

About the time you forgot
   your PE kit and cried
The time you wet yourself
   on the way to the loo (it *was* outside)
The time you kissed the girl
   on the school trip – the girl guide
And the time when you wouldn't
   tell on your mate, and you lied

Dad, I met someone who knew you
Dad, it was your old teacher from school
Dad, I've learned all sorts of things
    About you

Trevor Millum

My Grandpa

My grandpa is as round-shouldered
as a question mark
and is led about all day
by his walking stick.
With teeth that aren't real,
hidden behind a moustache that is,
while his memories simmer warmly
inside his crinkled paper bag of a face.

My grandpa,
old and worn on the outside,
sparky and fresh on the in.
For he often,
shakes my hand with fifty-pence pieces,
makes sweets pop out from behind his ears,
smokes all day like a train
then laughs like one as well.
Plays jokes on my mother
as he tries to freshen her face with a smile
and then tells me stories that electrify my brain.

But best of all,
when my dad loses his temper,
Grandpa just tells him
to sit down and behave himself!

Good old Grandpa!

Ian Souter

Ask No Questions

Ask no questions
Hear no lies
Our teacher's forgotten
To do up his flies!

Don't you look.
Don't you stare.
Teacher's wearing
Red underwear.

John Foster

My Mum Wears a Jelly Bra

My mum wears a jelly bra.
She says it helps her figure.
I reckon, she has matching pants
that make her bottom quiver.

Karen Costello-McFeat

Bathroom Blast Off

My dad has built a spaceship
In the bathroom of our home.
He's often off adventuring
And he always goes alone.

You know that he's time travelling
When he says, 'I'll be back soon'
But to us it seems like hours
That he spends inside that room!

He takes with him a book or two
And he blasts off once a day
When we hear the engine rasping
We know he's on his way.

I don't know if he meets friends there
'Cause my dad is such a loner
But if you sniff the bathroom when he's back
There's an alien aroma!

I've never seen his spaceship
But I know I can't be wrong
What other reason would he stay
In a bathroom for so long?

Kate Saunders

The Things That Get Caught in Our Teacher's Beard

It's sticky, it's slimy,
disgusting and weird,
the things that get caught in our teacher's beard.

Beans and spaghetti
caught heading south,
soggy rice crispies
that missed his mouth.

It's sticky, it's slimy,
disgusting and weird,
the things that get caught in our teacher's beard.

Old nail clippings
chewed from his toes,
bits of green stuff
blown from his nose.

It's sticky, it's slimy,
disgusting and weird,
the things that get caught in our teacher's beard.

Tomato sauce that drips from his chips,
froth from the coffee he noisily sips,
apple cores and orange pips,
pieces of chalk and paper clips.

It's sticky, it's slimy,
disgusting and weird,
the things that get caught in our teacher's beard.

Damian Harvey

Hairy Scary

My dad's a hairy, scary,
Started sprouting everywhere.
In every nook and cranny,
He's started growing hair.

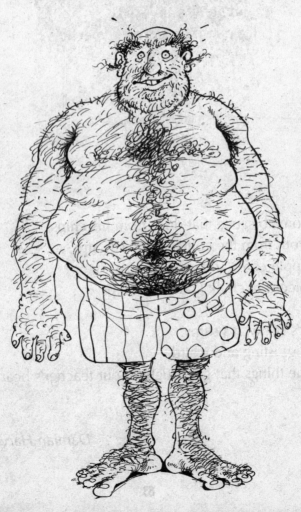

He's got hairy, scary nostrils
On his hairy, scary nose,
And despite his snipping, clipping it,
It grows and grows and grows.

He's got hairy, scary eyebrows,
And hairy, scary ears.
He doesn't need a trimmer
Needs a pair of garden shears.

He's hairy, scary everywhere,
Except, it must be said,
There's no hair where he wants it
On his oldy, baldy head.

Paul Bright

I'm Sorry

I'm sorry that I'm clever
I'm sorry that I'm bright.
I'm sorry I embarrass you
by choosing not to fight

in the playground after school
with Spig, the bully boy.
I'm sorry that I let you down.
I'm sorry I annoy.

I'm sorry that I'm swotty;
that I don't have a tattoo.
I'm sorry that I made you wince
at next door's barbecue

by quoting bits of Shakespeare,
and not passing on the chance
of finishing the evening
with a little ballet dance.

I'm sorry I'm peculiar,
for staying quiet for hours;
that my idea of happiness
is reading about flowers.

I'm sorry I can't skateboard.
I'm sorry for my size.
I'm sorry I find football
a pointless exercise.

I'm sorry I'm your first born;
that I don't make you glad.
I'm sorry you're not proud of me.
I'm really sorry, Dad.

Stewart Henderson

Broken

That vase with the flowers: she dropped it
in the kitchen. We heard the surprisingly
small crash and then that word also
slipped, or leaped from her lips, and broke
her rule, smashed on our ears. As we turned
she was standing stiff, shocked at the mess
made by the word splattered around her room.
At first she could not lift her eyes but when she did
they met ours burning helplessly
and then the tears burst

fragments
of glass, of water,
of memory, of heart

Dave Calder

Swimming Pool Palindrome

Really embarrassing!
Whoops!
Oh no . . .
Dad dived in
As trunks came down
Woosh! Splash! Aah! Splash! Splash!
Bottom bare!
Yikes!
Yikes!
Bare bottom!
Splash! Splash! Aah! Splash! Whoosh!
Down came trunks as
In dived Dad
　　　No! Oh . . .
　　　　Whoops!
　　　　　Embarrassing really!

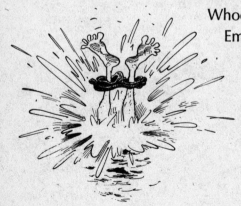

Paul Cookson